Wildlife in the City

in the CITY

Backyard Dwellers

Ellen Rodger

CRABTREE
PUBLISHING COMPANY
WWW.CRABTREEBOOKS.COM

Author: Ellen Rodger

Editorial director: Kathy Middleton

Art director: Rosie Gowsell Pattison

Editor: Petrice Custance

Proofreader: Wendy Scavuzzo

**Production coordinator and
 Prepress technician:** Ken Wright

Print coordinator: Katherine Berti

Images

Shutterstock.com: Thacho_kl: p28
(top right)

All other images
from Shutterstock

Produced for Crabtree Publishing
by Plan B Book Packagers
www.planbbookpackagers.com

Library and Archives Canada Cataloguing in Publication

Title: Backyard dwellers / Ellen Rodger.
Names: Rodger, Ellen, author.
Description: Series statement: Wildlife in the city | Includes index.
Identifiers: Canadiana (print) 20190128321 |
 Canadiana (ebook) 2019012833X |
 ISBN 9780778766889 (hardcover) |
 ISBN 9780778767046 (softcover) |
 ISBN 9781427124159 (HTML)
Subjects: LCSH: Urban animals—Juvenile literature. | LCSH: Urban
 pests—Juvenile literature. | LCSH: Urban ecology (Sociology)—Juvenile
 literature. | LCSH: Human-animal relationships. | LCSH: Nature—Effect of
 human beings on—Juvenile literature.
Classification: LCC QH541.5.C6 R64 2019 | DDC j591.75/6—dc23

Library of Congress Cataloging-in-Publication Data

Names: Rodger, Ellen, author.
Title: Backyard dwellers : abandoned and escaped animals / Ellen Rodger.
Description: New York : Crabtree Publishing Company, [2020] |
 Series: Wildlife in the city | Includes index.
Identifiers: LCCN 2019026944 (print) | LCCN 2019026945 (ebook) |
 ISBN 9780778766889 (hardcover) |
 ISBN 9780778767046 (paperback) |
 ISBN 9781427124159 (ebook)
Subjects: LCSH: Urban animals--North America--Juvenile literature.
Classification: LCC QH541.5.C6 R638 2020 (print) |
 LCC QH541.5.C6 (ebook) | DDC 591.75/6--dc23
LC record available at https://lccn.loc.gov/2019026944
LC ebook record available at https://lccn.loc.gov/2019026945

Crabtree Publishing Company

www.crabtreebooks.com   1-800-387-7650

Printed in the U.S.A./102019/CG20190809

**Published in Canada
Crabtree Publishing**
616 Welland Ave.
St. Catharines, Ontario
L2M 5V6

**Published in the United States
Crabtree Publishing**
PMB 59051
350 Fifth Avenue, 59th Floor
New York, New York 10118

**Published in the United Kingdom
Crabtree Publishing**
Maritime House
Basin Road North, Hove
BN41 1WR

**Published in Australia
Crabtree Publishing**
Unit 3–5 Currumbin Court
Capalaba
QLD 4157

CONTENTS

BACKYARD WILDLIFE

Humans aren't the only animals that like cozy homes in the city. There are plenty of wild animals that live near or with us. Often, they just blend into the background. Squirrels, for example, are some of the most common backyard animals in North America. They climb trees and dodge traffic on roads. People barely notice them, until they dig through and destroy gardens and flower beds. Then, these familiar **rodents** become annoying problems.

MEET MY "ASSOCIATE"

Wildlife live in all **urban** areas—even the most crowded cities. The urban wild animals that live closest to humans are called **associates** or **exploiters**. This is because they cleverly connect with or take advantage of human food sources. These sources include gardens and garbage. Exploiters use buildings, homes, and parks for protection and **denning** areas. Some common North American associates or exploiters include squirrels, raccoons, opossums, mice, and crows.

Toronto Wildlife Centre

Imagine rescuing wild animals as a job. Helping baby squirrels trapped in a building wall? All in a day's work! The Toronto Wildlife Centre (TWC) is the largest urban animal rescue in Canada. In addition to rescue work, it also has a hospital and **rehabilitation** center for injured and orphaned wild animals. The animals are cared for and when possible, released back into the wild. The goal is for the animals to survive on their own without human help. TWC is a **charity** that believes people and wildlife can coexist, or live peacefully near each other.

Depending on where you live in the world, exploiters can include armadillos, weasels, or even peregrine falcons.

5

HOME HABITAT

When it comes to some urban animals, your home and neighborhood is their home and neighborhood!

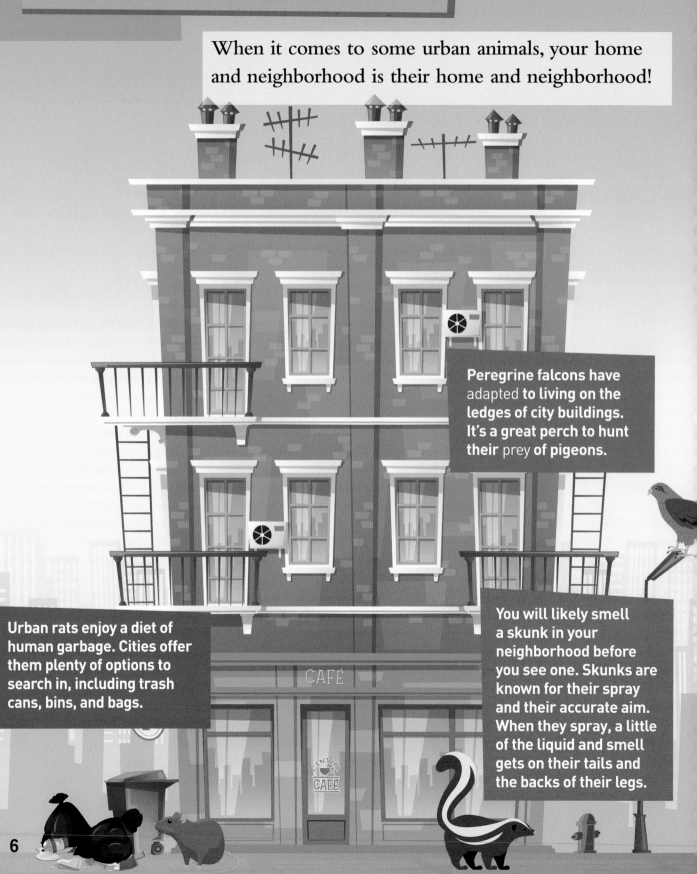

Peregrine falcons have adapted **to living on the ledges of city buildings. It's a great perch to hunt their** prey **of pigeons.**

Urban rats enjoy a diet of human garbage. Cities offer them plenty of options to search in, including trash cans, bins, and bags.

You will likely smell a skunk in your neighborhood before you see one. Skunks are known for their spray and their accurate aim. When they spray, a little of the liquid and smell gets on their tails and the backs of their legs.

CAFÉ

CENTRAL CAFÉ

Scientists have discovered that city rats eat better than country rats because their main meals come from our **protein**-rich garbage.

Squirrels will jump 20 feet (6 m) and perform high-wire acts to get at the nuts and seeds people put out for birds.

Birdfeeders are buffets for squirrels.

There's a raccoon living on every city block in North America. Some of them live in attics and crawlspaces.

Raccoons like areas with a lot of trees they can use for dens. They will also hole up in garages or sheds.

Skunks live in small burrows underneath the front porches of houses. They also like sheds and decks.

The common house mouse is a squatter. They like to squeeze through cracks and live in the basements of apartment buildings.

WHO GOES THERE?

Most humans—almost 55 percent of the world's population to be exact—live in or around urban areas. Urban areas include cities, towns, and villages. Our houses, parks, and apartment buildings were built on territory where animals live. And wherever we settle, our animal associates settle, too. It turns out that many animal **species** like to live near us.

BACKYARD BATTLEGROUND

Animal associates don't usually become a problem until they start messing with our ways of life. If there are too many in one area, or if they spread disease, humans view them as pests, or annoying animals. In 2018, raccoons with a deadly virus called distemper started showing up in parks in Brooklyn, New York. Locals began calling the sick animals "zombie raccoons" because they staggered around on their hind legs. Dozens of sick raccoons were rounded up and **euthanized**. WildlifeNYC is an organization that educates people on urban wildlife. It began instructing people not to feed raccoons and how to raccoon-proof their homes by blocking access routes.

Opossums are city scavengers who eat a lot of insect pests and dead animal remains. In turn, birds of prey such as hawks and owls feed on opossums.

Urban Biodiversity Monitoring

Some zoos are all about polar bears and penguins. Chicago's Lincoln Park Zoo is all that and more. The zoo has an Urban Wildlife Institute. This is an organization that studies how home and road building affects the urban **ecosystem**. The goal is to help humans coexist with urban animals. The Urban Wildlife Institute encourages people to learn about the animals that live around them. In one project, they asked people to identify animals in its urban wildlife photo collection. It has more than one million photos of Chicago wildlife.

The Urban Wildlife Institute has bat-monitoring stations at the zoo and in surrounding neighborhoods. Scientists keep track to see if the number of bats is decreasing. Citizens can help by telling where large bat colonies are located.

LE PEW

Skunks are helpful, but smelly, neighbors. In cities, skunks are feared for their "weapons system." Their stinky spray is their main natural defense against predators.

Skunks are nature's garbage disposal units and eat a lot of our trash.

If threatened, a skunk will stamp its front paws, lift its tail, and growl before it sprays.

Skunks live an average of three years on the streets and in neighborhoods.

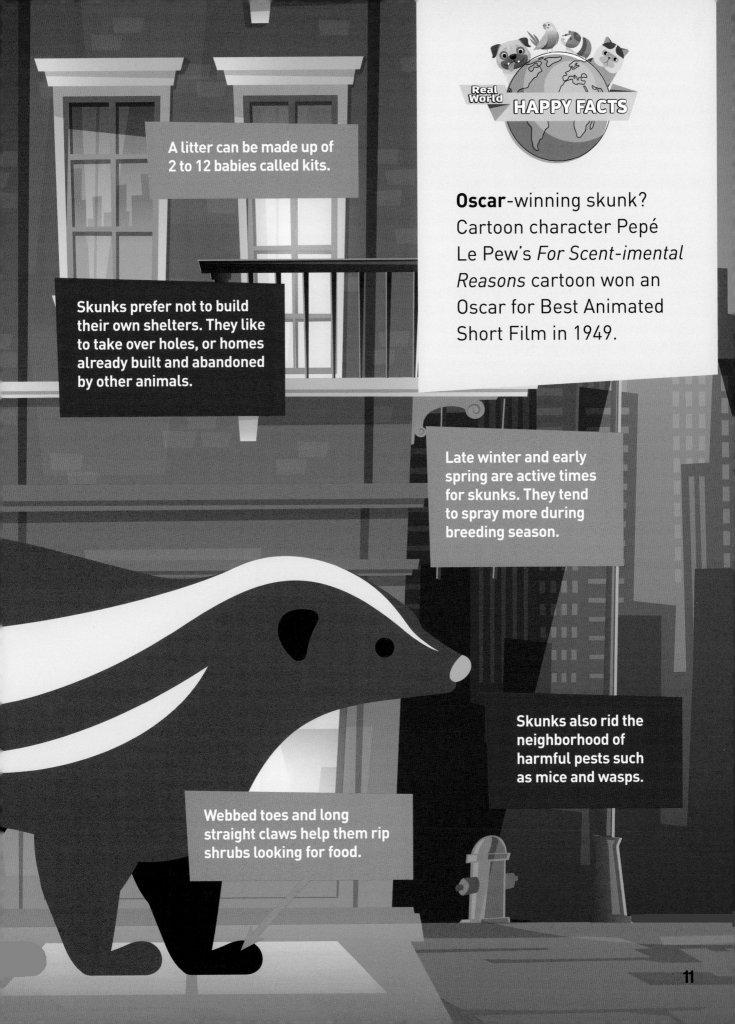

A litter can be made up of 2 to 12 babies called kits.

Skunks prefer not to build their own shelters. They like to take over holes, or homes already built and abandoned by other animals.

Oscar-winning skunk? Cartoon character Pepé Le Pew's *For Scent-imental Reasons* cartoon won an Oscar for Best Animated Short Film in 1949.

Late winter and early spring are active times for skunks. They tend to spray more during breeding season.

Skunks also rid the neighborhood of harmful pests such as mice and wasps.

Webbed toes and long straight claws help them rip shrubs looking for food.

RACCOON RACKET

Masked bandit, night raider, trash panda... Judging by the nasty nicknames people give them, raccoons don't get a lot of respect. This is because, in urban areas, they make a lot of mess when they break into trash cans while looking for a meal.

Raccoons are smart and sturdy adaptors.

They will tear up a lawn to get a meal of grubs.

They live in urban, rural, and forested areas of North and South America.

Raccoons have litters of three to four babies.

Raccoons are very smart and great problem solvers.

As scavengers, they clean up the environment by eating pests and rodents.

Moviegoers love cartoon and animatronic, or lifelike robotic, raccoons. Rocket, from the *Guardians of the Galaxy* movies, RJ from *Over the Hedge*, and Meeko from *Pocahontas* are famous for their slightly cranky personalities.

They have poor vision (during the day) but an excellent sense of smell.

They like to make dens in the attics of houses and will enter houses through uncapped chimneys.

They use their long fingers and nails to open trash cans.

AWESOME OPOSSUM

Opossums have pouches! In fact, they are the only pouched mammal in the United States and Canada. These **marsupials** are attracted to the ready meals they find in urban areas. They aren't picky about dumpster diving or eating dead animals.

Oppossums kill ticks, which is good for humans and other animals. Some ticks spread diseases.

Opossums eat snakes, birds, insects, grass, fruit, and nuts. Persimmons and pet food are said to be favorite foods.

Opossums make their nests in dens made by other animals. Some also live in tree holes or under porches and in attics.

Opossums can play dead when threatened. Commonly called "playing possum," this behavior sometimes happens when they are frightened. If bluffing doesn't work, they will also hiss and bare their 50 teeth.

Opossums are often called "possums" which may confuse people who live in Australia. There, possums are small brown marsupials.

Older babies sometimes ride on their mother's back.

Female opossums give birth to as many as 20 young. They are tiny and helpless when born and immediately crawl into their mother's pouch to develop.

The North American opossum is also known as the Virginia opossum.

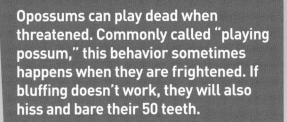

INVASION OF THE VERMIN

Urban rats have a bad reputation, but not without some cause. City-loving black and Norway rats can spread diseases that are harmful to people, including **salmonella** food poisoning. We try very hard to rid our homes and cities of rats by using traps and poisons. But these incredible adapters go wherever humans go, and can develop a **resistance** to some poisons.

In 1948, pest control services in North America started used a poison called Warfarin. When eaten by rats, it prevented their blood from clotting. They then bled to death. By 1958, city rats and mice had adapted to Warfarin, making them immune *to it.*

BIG CITY RATS

New York City has more than two million rats. That's more rats than people! Since 2017, it has been waging war on its rat population. The biggest weapons? Starvation and **extermination**. The city hires rat catchers and has tried to make garbage harder for rats to get into. Paris, France is also crawling with rats. The city launched a rat removal program called "Le Smash" where people were encouraged to do their part in trapping and removing rats. But the rats have fans, too. Some people like them and say they are "environmentally friendly" because they eat trash.

Look Around You

Rats are crafty at finding a free meal. To keep them and other critters out of your cereal box, you need to develop a rat's eye for food and lodging. Grab a notepad and inspect your home the way a rat-control professional would. Make your own report on rat security.

1   Take note of entry points, including holes in baseboards.

2   Check how your food is stored. Is it in a sealed container? Could a rat get into it?

3   Is garbage kept tightly sealed indoors and out?

4   Have you noticed any signs of vermin visits, such as droppings on countertops and floors?

AW, RATS!

Rats are probably our most feared urban animal. Humans have a long history of living near and with them.

A rat can squish through a hole less than 1 inch (2.5 cm) wide.

Norway rats breed throughout the year and have litters of about seven babies. The babies are on their own after four weeks.

They build their dens underground with long tunnels and food storage areas.

Their tails have no fur and help them to control their body temperatures.

Rats use their tails for balance when climbing or walking along wires or branches.

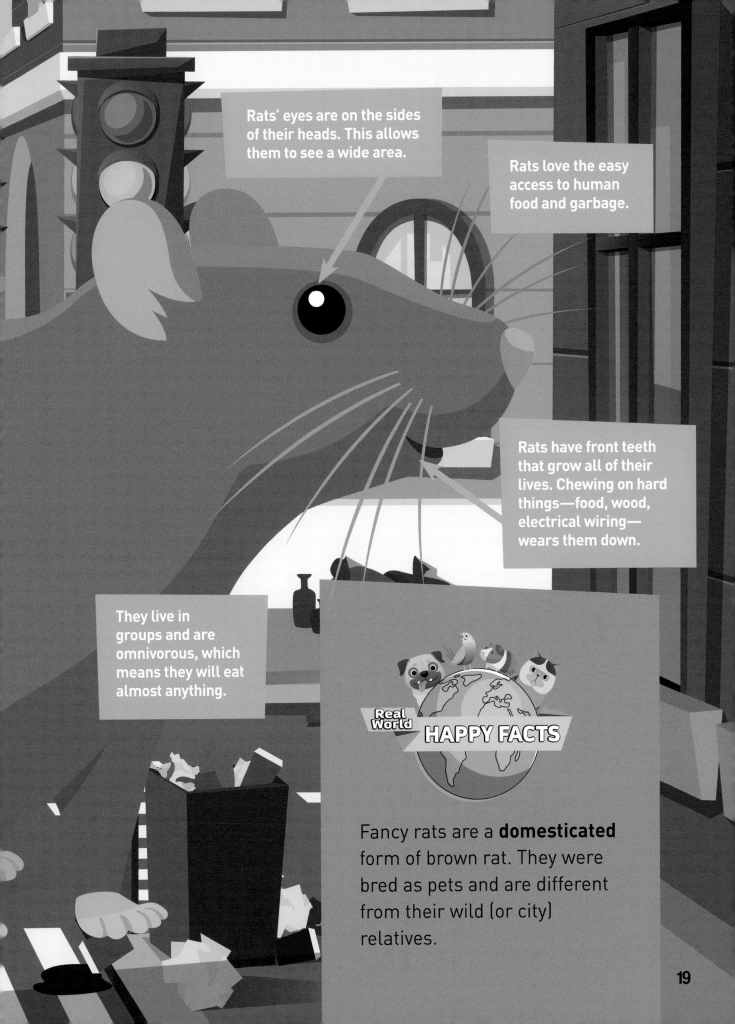

Rats' eyes are on the sides of their heads. This allows them to see a wide area.

Rats love the easy access to human food and garbage.

Rats have front teeth that grow all of their lives. Chewing on hard things—food, wood, electrical wiring—wears them down.

They live in groups and are omnivorous, which means they will eat almost anything.

Real World HAPPY FACTS

Fancy rats are a **domesticated** form of brown rat. They were bred as pets and are different from their wild (or city) relatives.

DRIVING ME NUTS

Squirrels are nuts for nuts—and plant bulbs, and seeds, and a whole bunch of other things in the urban back or front yard. That's why these furry rodents ruffle the feathers of city gardeners. Plant a pretty tulip bulb and squirrels will dig it up for a meal. For the most part, humans and squirrels live together in harmony. Most problems arise when squirrels make the inside of our homes their homes.

They skitter through city parks and streets, and leap onto apartment balconies. Squirrels are well adapted to urban life and can climb brick surfaces and poles just as well as they climb trees.

IT'S A SQUIRREL STAMPEDE!

When we built our cities, we were building on squirrel territory. Forests covered much of eastern North America hundreds of years ago. At that time, eastern gray squirrels were known to **migrate**. In a good acorn year, squirrels had two litters of babies. The population explosion usually resulted in millions of squirrels heading south for food. The migrations happened several times from the 1800s through to the late 1990s. Today, many of these squirrels are city-dwellers. City squirrels get plenty of food from nut trees, fruit, and gardens. They have adapted to scavenge through garbage and raid bird feeders for seeds.

Look Around You: Squirrels in your Schoolyard

Look around your neighborhood or schoolyard. What kinds of squirrels do you see? Are they gray, black, or red? Try watching for squirrels for an hour and writing down the number and colors of squirrels you see. The website squirrelmapper.org asks ordinary people to help with squirrel research by observing the squirrels in their neighborhoods and sharing the information. Teachers and parents can register with SquirrelMapper and download data recording sheets.

GOING SQUIRRELLY

Squirrels are among the most well-known and visible wildlife in cities. It is a safe bet that you have dozens living near you right now.

Squirrels have four large front teeth for chewing and gnawing. These constantly grow. Their cheek teeth are used for grinding food.

Squirrels eat nuts, seeds, fruit, leafy vegetables, and insects.

Their claws help them grasp while climbing. They love to climb.

They mate once or twice a year and make nests in trees or sometimes in the attics of homes.

Washington, D.C.'s black squirrels are a gift from Canada. Eight black squirrels were given to the National Zoo in 1902 as part of a gray-for-black squirrel exchange. The Canadian squirrels came from Rondeau Provincial Park in southern Ontario. The park received several eastern gray squirrels. Black squirrels and gray squirrels are the same species but with different-colored fur. The **descendants** of both the black and the gray squirrels are thriving today.

Squirrels are rodents. They belong to the same family as mice, beavers, hamsters, and porcupines.

Nests are called dreys or dens. They are made of twigs, leaves, and other soft material a squirrel might find.

A squirrel's hind legs are longer than their front legs.

THE URBAN BIRD

Many birds do well in cities. Cities offer plenty of food, perches, and shelter. Bird lovers buy more than $3 billion in seed to feed wild birds every year in the U.S. They may think they are doing the birds a favor, but ornithologists, or bird scientists, say that's not true. Most of the birds that gather for a meal at urban bird feeders are **invasive species** such as sparrows and pigeons.

Peregrine falcons are birds of prey. They have become common in cities where fat meals such as pigeons are numerous. They sometimes nest on tall buildings.

Cats, pesticides, and window reflections are threats to urban birds. An estimated 100 million birds die each year when they fly into windows.

Not for the (Local) Birds

Studies show urban birdfeeders crowd out native birds. They also attract animals that prey on birds, such as cats and raccoons. Instead of spreading out a buffet at a feeder, ornithologists suggest that people create natural bird **habitats**. This means planting trees and plants with leaves that attract insects. Insects are much better meals for birds.

BIRD TAKEOVER

House sparrows and European starlings are European birds released in North America more than 100 years ago. It seemed like a good idea at the time. People thought the birds looked nice. But they have been taking over **native** birds ever since. A few starlings were introduced in New York's Central Park in the 1800s. Today, there are more than 200 million. Like many birds, starlings pick at trash cans for meals. They build their nests in holes, including exhaust fan vents.

SOMETHING TO CROW ABOUT

Crows are smart birds that have adapted well to cities. They are so smart that they know when garbage day is in your neighborhood. It's true! On collection days, urban crows show up for the easy pickings.

Crows are omnivorous, meaning they will eat almost anything.

Crow predators include birds of prey such as red-tailed hawks, peregrine falcons, owls, and eagles.

They hide their nests of twigs and animal hair in tree branches. They lay three to nine eggs that they sit on for 16 to 18 days.

There are about 40 different crow species around the world.

Crows can use tools such as hooked sticks to dig out food from hard-to-reach places.

Crows have long memories and can hold a grudge. If you treat them poorly, they will remember you and may call angrily at you. They can remember a face for decades.

Crow eggs are blue-green to olive green, with blotches of brown and gray.

They help to keep the environment clean by eating dead animals and garbage.

Real World HAPPY FACTS

Puy du Fou theme park in France has trained crows to pick up garbage. Six birds were hand-raised and given treats when they picked up cigarette butts. Now they work at the park four days a week.

BACKYARD BANDICOOT

Imagine having a monkey living on your balcony. How about a baboon or a bandicoot in your back shed? Around the world, animals that were once wild are now living in cities. Many have had to adapt to city life because of urban sprawl. Urban sprawl happens when cities outgrow their spaces and expand into nearby countryside.

Bandicoots dig up lawn grass to get their meals, but they also snack on funnel web spiders. This makes them a form of insect control.

SLOW DOWN for **BANDICOOTS**

Caution shared path

What does backyard wildlife look like in other areas of the world? In Cape Town, South Africa, chacma baboons are known for stealing fruit and damaging cars. In Rio de Janeiro, Brazil, large rodents called capybaras live in some city parks.

BRAKE FOR BANDICOOTS

A bandicoot is a small marsupial that looks like an overgrown hamster with a long nose. These Australian animals are commonly seen in woodlands and backyards. They have a taste for grubs, so they are attracted to gardens and grass lawns. Habitat fragmentation, or the break up of their natural living space, has shrunk bandicoot populations. This fragmentation happens when cities grow and houses are built on their territories.

Urban Biodiversity Inventory

When cities sprawl, animals either disappear or alter how they live. Biologists in Sao Paulo, Brazil conducted a biodiversity inventory to track changes. A biodiversity inventory is a detailed list of the types of animals and plants found in a specific area. The list revealed 1,113 wild animal species live in the city. Wildlife experts and city workers compiled the information for more than 20 years. The city's parks and **green spaces** are home to adaptors such as toucans, marmosets, jaguars, and sloths. Their habitat has been swallowed up by urban sprawl.

The inventory found that birds such as toucans use the city's trees as stopovers to forests.

LEARNING MORE

Books

Bodden, Valerie. *Skunks.* Creative Paperbacks, 2016.

Carney, Elizabeth. *Animals in the City.* National Geographic Children's Books, 2019.

Kalman, Bobbie. *Living Things in my Backyard.* Crabtree Publishing, 2008.

Read, Tracy. *Exploring the World of Raccoons.* Firefly Books, 2010.

Websites

www.inaturalist.org/projects/l-a-nature-map
The Natural History Museum Los Angeles County has a nature map of L.A.'s wildlife. You can search it for specific animals and add your own observations.

www.virtualmuseum.ca/sgc-cms/expositions-exhibitions/
faune_urbaine-urban_wildlife/accueil-home-eng.php
This site has an urban wildlife section with cool games.

https://vetmed.illinois.edu/wildlifeencounters/
index.html
This site includes lessons for different grade levels on habitats and humans relating to wildlife.

www.torontowildlifecentre.com
Visit this site to learn how an urban wildlife center operates.

GLOSSARY

adapted Changed or became used to new conditions

associates Animals that find food in cities and towns, including in garbage and gardens

charity An organization that raises money to help humans or animals

denning Digging holes or finding spaces in which to raise babies

descendants Relatives of a person or animal who lived at an earlier time

domesticated Describing animals that are tame or live closely with humans

ecosystem A community of living things and their physical environment

euthanized Put to death humanely, or without causing pain

extermination The killing of a group of animals

exploiters Animals that live around humans to get some benefit, such as food or places to make their homes

green spaces Areas of grass, trees, and other plants that are in or around urban areas such as cities

habitats The natural environments of living things

immune Resistant to something

invasive species Animals or plants that live in an environment that is not their natural home, and often cause harm to it

marsupials Mammals that carry their young in a pouch on their bodies

migrate To move from one habitat or region to another

native Belonging to, or originating in, a specific area

Oscar The nickname of the golden statuette given to Academy Award winners in the movie industry

prey Animals that are hunted and killed by other animals for food

protein A nutrient found in foods such as meat, eggs, milk, and legumes

rehabilitation Helping an injured or sick animal get well and return to its normal life

resistance The lack of sensitivity to something as a result of a genetic change or continued exposure

rodents Animals, such as rats, mice, squirrels, and porcupines, that gnaw because they have constantly growing front teeth

salmonella A bacterium that causes intestinal infection

scavengers Animals that feed on garbage or dead animals

species A group of similar plants or animals that can breed with one another

squatters People or animals that occupy land or a building that is not theirs

urban Relating to cities or towns

INDEX

QUESTIONS & ANSWERS

Q: Skunks are so cute. Can I have one as a pet?

A: In general, it is best to let wild animals be wild. They will live better lives in the wild. Wild skunks should never be pets.

Q: How can I help animal associates?

A: If they are not causing harm, the best thing you can do is leave them alone. Don't feed them. Animal associates are survivors. They can find enough food on their own. You can also educate other people about how important they are. One opossum alone can kill 5,000 ticks a year!